ANIMAL BUILDERS

Written by Jenny Wood

Illustrated by
Mike Atkinson, Jim Channell,
Robert Cook and Terry Riley

HAMLYN

Published in 1992 by
Hamlyn Children's Books,
part of Reed International Books,
Michelin House, 81 Fulham Road,
London SW3 6RB

Copyright © Reed International Books Ltd 1992

All rights reserved. No part of the publication may be reproduced, stored in a retrieval system, or transmitted, in any form or by any means, electronic, mechanical, photocopying, recording or otherwise, without the prior permission of the copyright holders

Produced for Hamlyn Children's Books by Oyster Books

Consultant: Dr Julian Hector

Design: Designworks!, Cheltenham

ISBN 0 600 57356 7

Paper Back ISBN 0 600 57686 8

Printed in Belgium

Contents

Introduction **5**
The North American Beaver **6**
The Rufous Ovenbird **8**
The Magnetic Termite **10**
The Weaver Ant **12**
The Caddis Fly Larva **14**
The Three-Spined Stickleback **16**
The Orb-Weaver Spider **18**
The Satin Bowerbird **20**
The Common Wasp **22**
The European Water Spider **24**
The Masked Weaver Bird **26**
The Black-Tailed Prairie Dog **28**
The Trapdoor Spider **30**
The Mallee Fowl **32**
The Malaysian Cave Swiftlet **34**
The European Common Mole **36**
The Grey Tree Frog **38**
The Rainbow Parrot Fish **40**
The Southern Hairy-Nosed Wombat **42**
The Potter Wasp **44**
The 'Gardening' Ant **46**
Glossary **48**
Index **48**

Introduction

Humans are usually considered to be the world's greatest builders, but there are other members of the animal kingdom who construct far more intricate and complicated structures using a range of remarkable skills and often extraordinary strength.

Animal builders come in all shapes and sizes, and are found in different habitats all over the world. Some build alone. Others organize themselves into groups or teams to build immense structures which are gigantic in comparison to the size of the builders themselves.

Animal builders are skilful creatures. They can chew, weave, dig, tunnel, decorate and design. Some can even make their own building materials. Termites mix their saliva with earth to produce a kind of soft cement. Wasps mix their saliva with chewed wood to produce a substance which dries into a type of paper. Spiders and some ants have glands in their bodies which can produce silk for weaving. Other animal builders make use of whatever building materials they can find nearby.

While humans have had to invent special tools to help them build, many other animal builders are able to use parts of their bodies as tools. These body parts have developed in ways that allow the creatures to build cleverly and efficiently. Powerful feet and claws, strong teeth and curved beaks, for example, are all designed to make an animal builder's work much easier.

Animal builders do not build for fun. All their structures are made for a purpose. Some are built as traps for prey, others as places where the builder can court a mate. Some are designed as nests where developing eggs can be kept warm until they are ready to hatch. The most elaborate structures act as fortresses, built for the protection of the individual builder, or perhaps for a whole colony of creatures. These fortresses often provide places where animal builders can bring up their young in safety, away from the attention of enemies and the danger of possible attack. They may be immense buildings, with a whole network of tunnels and rooms. They may have air conditioning, drains, food stores, nurseries for the young, even gardens.

By building their amazing structures, animal builders improve their chances of surviving in a dangerous and hostile world.

The North American Beaver

Crash! The cool stillness of the forest is suddenly shattered by the sound of a young tree falling to the ground. A small, brown, furry creature scurries through the undergrowth and slips into the nearby river for safety. It waits there until it is sure that no enemies have been attracted by the noise, then returns to the tree. Its strong front teeth set to work gnawing through the branches, stripping the trunk bare. The North American beaver then grasps the trunk in its powerful jaws and drags it into the water. The creature tugs and pushes the trunk into position amongst the mound of branches, twigs, mud and boulders which make up its dam.

North American beavers live in rivers and freshwater lakes in woodland areas. They eat tree bark, twigs, leaves, the roots of trees and shrubs, and water plants such as water lilies. When they dive, their ears and nostrils close to keep water out, and a transparent covering slides down over each eye to allow them to see underwater.

Beavers are expert builders, and extremely hard-working. A dam may be more than 300 metres long, and the help of several beaver families may be required to build it! First, sticks and branches are thrust into the river bed. The trunks of young trees are laid across the branches, and weighed down with boulders. Mud is then scooped up from the river bed and pushed in amongst the branches and stones to bind the whole dam together. The dam provides the beaver with a living area which is safe from enemies such as bears and lynxes, as well as a place to store food for the winter. In the water behind the dam, the beaver then builds a home called a lodge.

A beaver has 20 teeth. The four strong, curved front teeth are called incisors, and are used for gnawing through the trunks of trees. The 16 back teeth are used for chewing. A beaver's incisors have a bright orange outer covering, and never wear out. Between the incisors and the back teeth are flaps of skin, one on each side of the beaver's mouth. These flaps fold inwards, and seal off the back of the mouth to prevent splinters of wood or water entering the beaver's lungs.

A beaver's paddle-like tail is covered with scales. The beaver uses its tail to steer through the water, and as a support when it stands on its hind legs to gnaw at the trunk of a tree. If a beaver senses danger, it slaps its tail on the water to warn others.

The dome-shaped lodge is built from branches, reeds and mud. The only way in is through an underwater tunnel. Inside is a living chamber, the floor of which lies about 15 centimetres above the water. Here the beaver family can live safely. Nearby, the beavers keep an underwater store of branches and logs to eat during the cold winter months.

The Rufous Ovenbird

The rain falls steadily but, for the Rufous ovenbirds, this is ideal nest-building weather. They hop across the soggy ground, gathering mud, grass and straw. When they can hold no more in their beaks, the birds fly to a nearby fence post and begin to build their oven-shaped nest. At last the nest shape is complete, but the ovenbirds' task is not quite over. They must make the nest completely safe. Just inside, behind the entrance hole, they build a mud wall. High on this wall, carefully placed so that it is not opposite the outside entrance hole, the birds make another hole, just large enough for them to pass through. Behind this lies the nesting chamber, lined with grass.

Rufous ovenbirds live in the South American countries of Brazil, Argentina and Paraguay. They are often seen near houses and roadsides, and will build their nests in the open, on fence posts, or under the eaves of houses. Their nickname is the 'baker', because the nests they build look rather like old-fashioned ovens. Rufous ovenbirds build a new nest every year, but their old nests, baked hard by the hot sun, are sturdy and often stay in place for two or three years. They may be used by other birds such as swallows.

Rufous ovenbirds usually build their nests out in the open, and so must make them safe from other animals and birds who might want to steal the eggs. They do this by building an inner wall inside the nest. This inner wall faces the entrance hole to the nest and keeps the eggs hidden from view. The wall also creates a short passageway, at the end of which is a bend. The ovenbirds are able to move along the passageway and round the bend to reach the eggs at the heart of the nest, but it is almost impossible for other predators to reach inside.

A male and female Rufous ovenbird often stay together for life. They help each other build their nest and share the tasks of incubating the eggs and looking after the chicks once they are hatched.

The Magnetic Termite

It is dawn. The rising sun strikes the eastern side of the giant termite mound, gently warming it. Inside the mound, the worker termites move through the maze of tunnels and galleries, seeking the warmth of the eastern chambers. Some carry out repairs to the walls of the chambers, making a kind of cement from earth mixed with their own saliva. Others, guarded by a strong force of soldier termites, leave the nest to hunt for food. Deep inside the mound, below ground level, the bloated queen termite is also hard at work, laying eggs. With her is her king. Both queen and king are cleaned and fed by a court of workers. Other workers carry the eggs to the nursery chambers and tend the developing larvae.

Most termites live underground or inside dead wood, but some species, such as the magnetic termite found in Australia, build huge mounds which can be over seven metres high. Termites die if they become too hot or too cold, so the mound-building termites have developed ways of preventing the temperature inside the mound from rising too high during the day or falling too low at night. The magnetic termites' solution is to build high, wedge-shaped mounds. The wide, flat surfaces of the wedge face east and west, and so get the gentle heat of the morning or evening sun. At midday, the fierce heat of the sun hits only the narrow edge of the wedge, and so the inside of the mound does not overheat.

Chambers inside a termite mound are used as food stores and as nurseries for the larvae. A queen termite may lay as many as 30,000 eggs each day, so the nursery chambers are often full! Termites mostly eat wood and dead plant material.

The walls of a termite mound are made from earth mixed with saliva. The termites chew pellets of earth until they become like soft cement. These pellets are then stuck together and left to harden.

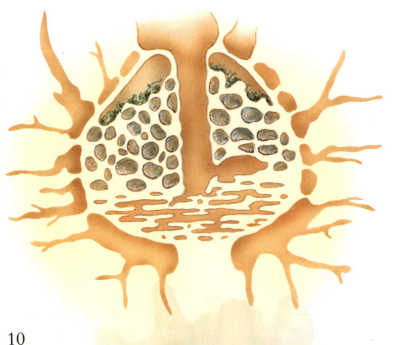

Termites live in huge colonies, some of which can contain as many as seven million members!

The shape of the magnetic termites' mound, and the way in which it is built so that the thin ends face north and south, and the wide ends east and west, help control the temperature inside. The termites obtain just the right amount of heat from the sun at the right times.

Inside the mound.

The Weaver Ant

High among the branches, thousands of weaver ants are hard at work building their home. The larger worker ants use their legs and jaws to pull the edges of two leaves together. Smaller worker ants, carrying ant larvae in their jaws, move steadily down the joint between the two leaves. These workers gently squeeze the larvae which squirt out thin strands of sticky silk. Before long, the two leaves are stuck firmly together. The larger workers release their grip and move to the next pair of leaves. Soon the team of ants have glued enough leaves together to make the leafy ball which will be their nest.

Ants are found in almost every part of the world, except at the Poles. They are social insects which live in large groups called colonies. Colonies can contain over a million members. Many species of ant live underground, but the weaver ants of Australia and Africa live in trees. These ants have gripping claws on their legs which help them climb trees and hold on to leaves. Weaver ant larvae can produce silk, and the adults use this silk to help build their nests. Most ants have a sting which they use to defend themselves. The weaver ant gives a particularly painful sting by squirting formic acid into the wound it makes.

The silk which the workers squeeze from the larvae sticks the leaves of the nest together. This 'weaving' skill gives the ants their name.

An ant's jaws are known as mandibles. They move from side to side, rather than up and down. Weaver ants have very powerful mandibles. They use their mandibles to pull leaves together and to hold the larvae, while building their leafy nest. Ants use their sensitive antennae to smell, touch, taste and hear.

The finished weaver ant nest is a ball of leaves. If the nest is disturbed, the ants inside tap the leaves, making a rattling sound which frightens away the enemy. Thousands of weaver ants will live together in a single nest.

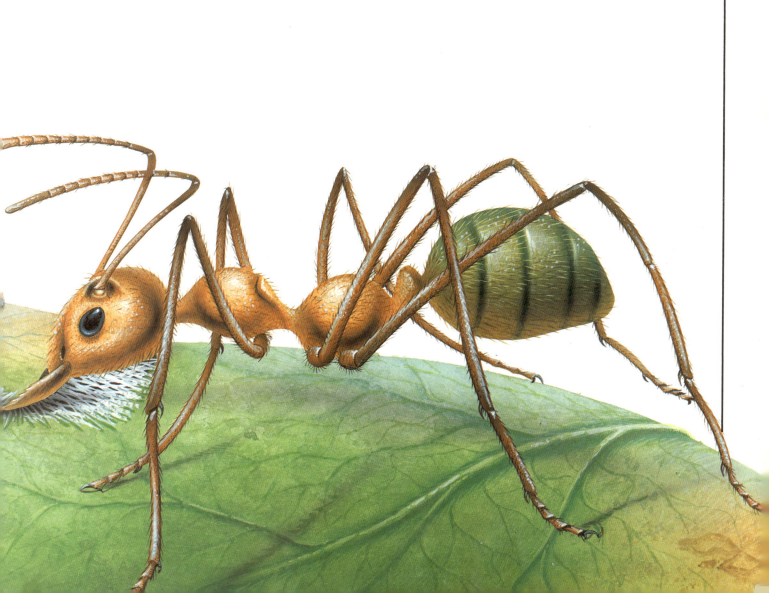

The Caddis Fly Larva

The slow-moving water of the stream is clear and clean. Hidden behind a rock, out of sight of predators, the caterpillar-like caddis fly larva builds its home. A gland near the larva's mouth produces sticky silk which the larva winds around its body. Reaching out with its front legs, the larva then makes a collection of objects such as grains of sand, shells, small stones, dead leaf fragments and tiny twigs. The larva pulls these objects towards it and presses them, one by one, on to the sticky silk. Eventually the larva's mobile home is complete, perfectly camouflaged by the objects stuck to the outside.

Caddis fly larvae have soft, caterpillar-like bodies which make them easy prey for predators. The cases the larvae build around their bodies only partly protect them, because many fish will eat them — case and all!

Caddis flies are found almost everywhere in the world where there is fresh water. Adult caddis flies look like, and are closely related to, moths. Female caddis flies lay their eggs on stones or plants either near or under water. The eggs hatch into larvae, which live under water for about a year before developing into adults. Many species of caddis fly larvae build protective cases around their bodies. The larva's head and front legs stick out from the front end of the case, so that the larvae can move through the water easily in search of food.

Each species of caddis fly can be identified by the particular shape of the case it makes, and the objects with which the case is covered.

This caddis fly larva lives in very slow-moving water. It builds its case from the shells of snails and other small water creatures.

This caddis fly larva uses sand grains and twigs for its case. The jutting-out twigs give extra protection because the case is a very difficult shape for a fish to swallow.

The largest type of caddis fly larva makes its protective case by winding pieces of plant material around its body in a spiral.

Some caddis fly larvae, which live in fast-moving water, do not move around. Instead, they weave a silken net around their body for protection and attach the net to the underside of a stone or plant.

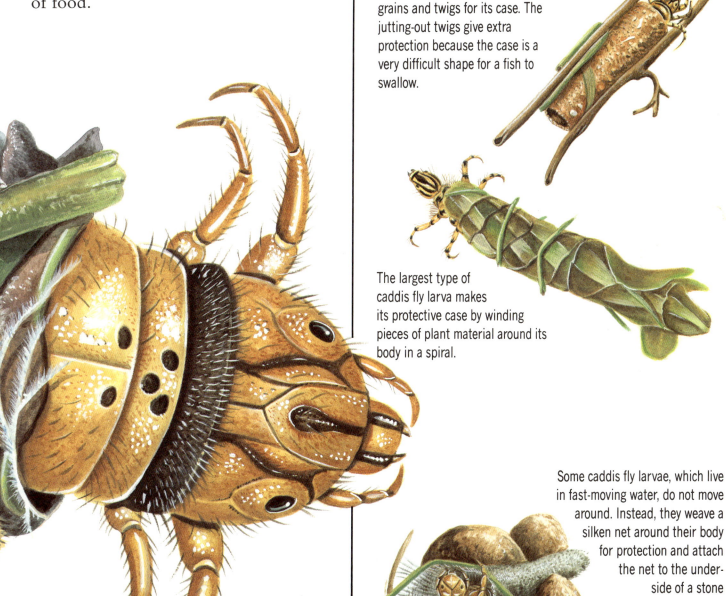

The Three-Spined Stickleback

The male three-spined stickleback darts to the bottom of the stream. He sucks up sand in his mouth then, with a few strokes of his tail, moves away from the nest site and spits out the sand. Soon he has hollowed out a pit in the bed of the stream. He then collects small pieces of water plant in his mouth, carries them back to the nest site and piles them into the pit. Pressing his stomach against the plants, he binds them together into a solid mass with a sticky substance produced from his kidneys. The stickleback charges at the mound, butting it into shape, then forces his way right through the mound to make a tunnel. The nest is ready. All the stickleback needs to do now is find a suitable female!

There are eight species of stickleback, which are found in most fresh and coastal waters in the northern half of the world. The three-spined stickleback lives in the Pacific and Atlantic Oceans around the coasts of America and Western Europe, but moves into freshwater rivers and streams to breed. All stickleback nests are built by the male fish who then fiercely defend their territories from other males. When the eggs hatch, the male stickleback looks after the young fish, which are called fry. Each male will have several families in one breeding season.

Three-spined sticklebacks are usually found in a stream or river where water plants grow freely. As well as providing male three-spined sticklebacks with material for their nests, these plants also act as hiding places when the fish are in danger of being attacked. Three-spined sticklebacks are not strong swimmers. After a period of heavy rain, they may shelter amongst the water plants to avoid being swept along by the fast-flowing current.

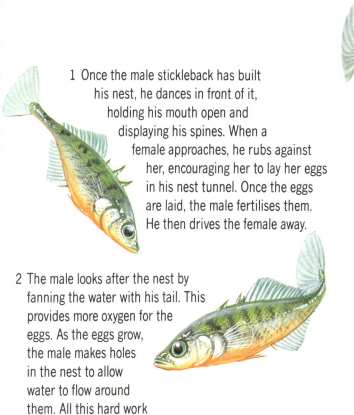

1 Once the male stickleback has built his nest, he dances in front of it, holding his mouth open and displaying his spines. When a female approaches, he rubs against her, encouraging her to lay her eggs in his nest tunnel. Once the eggs are laid, the male fertilises them. He then drives the female away.

2 The male looks after the nest by fanning the water with his tail. This provides more oxygen for the eggs. As the eggs grow, the male makes holes in the nest to allow water to flow around them. All this hard work causes the bright colours of the male stickleback's scales to fade.

3 The fry hatch after about eight days. The male looks after them. If they try to wander off, he grabs them in his mouth and spits them back into the nest. Once the fry are about two weeks old, they are able to look after themselves.

The male three-spined stickleback builds a bigger and more spectacular nest than any of the other species of stickleback. As he prepares to breed, the throat and chest of the male three-spined stickleback become deep red, and his eyes bright blue.

The Orb-Weaver Spider

The orb-weaver spider begins to spin its beautiful, intricate web between two flower stems. Each of its silk glands produces a different kind of silk, and the spider uses a mixture of these to create its web. Several threads of dry silk radiate out from the centre of the web like the spokes of a wheel. A short length of dry silk coils around the centre to hold the spokes firmly in place. The spider then spins a spiralling line of sticky silk to act as a trap. Once the web is complete, the spider removes the short length of dry silk and eats it to conserve its silk supply. Finally it attaches a long thread of silk to the web's centre and returns to its nest trailing this length behind it. The trap is set.

The orb-weaver spider builds its web across a favourite route used by flying insects. Its nest is usually spun on a folded leaf, and is always close by the web. The spider hides inside its nest, holding the trap line which it has attached to the web. When an insect lands in the web, the line vibrates, and the spider darts out to capture its prey which it then wraps in sheets of silk to prevent it from escaping. Many orb-weaver spiders spin a new web every night, a process which takes them about an hour. Before they do this they eat the silk from their old web so as not to waste the valuable protein it contains. Others repair or replace damaged parts of their webs.

Spinning an orb web

1 The spider floats a line of silk between two flower stems.

2 More lines of silk are spun to create a Y shape. This acts as the centre of the web.

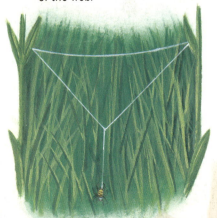

3 Other threads are then attached to the centre of the web, like the spokes of a wheel.

4 A line of dry silk is coiled around the centre of the web to hold the spokes in place.

Finally, the spider spins a line of sticky silk. This is the silk that traps insects for the spider to eat.

Orb-weaver spiders build the most beautiful and complicated of all webs. These are often woven between tree branches or flower stems. An orb web can contain as much as 20 metres of silk.

The Satin Bowerbird

The male satin bowerbird is busy on the forest floor. He clears an area of ground then carpets it with a layer of sticks and twigs. In the centre of this he builds two parallel walls of upright sticks, using his beak to weave the twigs together. This structure is called a bower. When the building work is finished, the bowerbird decorates the ground in front of his bower with a mass of brightly-coloured flowers, shells, leaves, fruit and pebbles. The bird even makes a kind of paint from crushed flowers, fruit and leaves mixed with saliva. Holding a piece of tree bark in his beak as a brush, he paints the inside walls of the bower. When all the decorations are complete, the bower is ready for use.

Bowerbirds live mainly in Papua New Guinea and northern Australia. There are several different species which all build different-shaped bowers. The satin bowerbird is one of a group known as 'avenue builders'. The bowers are used as places where the male birds perform courtship dances to attract a mate. Once the male has finished building and decorating his bower, he sits on a nearby branch and sings. When a mate appears, the male dances in his bower.

The tooth-billed bowerbird clears an area of forest floor to make an open stage. He carpets this with large, fresh leaves which he cuts from certain trees then places upside-down on the ground so that their pale undersides stand out against the dark earth.

'Maypole-building' bowerbirds use small trees to support the towers, arches or pyramids they build from twigs. One of these maypole-builders, MacGregor's bowerbird, builds a single tower. Around the tower's base, the bird builds a low-walled track in which he dances.

The Common Wasp

The worker wasps swarm over the rotting branch. They chew the wood with their mouthparts, mixing it with saliva to make a soft cement, then fly back to the nest. Some rush to the outer wall where they spit out the wood cement, laying it along the rim to form the nest's skin. The sun soon dries the cement into a tough, light paper. Other wasps work on the cells which make up the inside of the nest. As they lay the wood pulp in place, they use their antennae to measure the angles and thickness of the walls to create a regular pattern of six-sided cells. As the workers finish, the queen begins to lay her eggs.

'Social' wasps live in huge colonies. Most species build their many-celled nests out of paper, although some use mud. The nests may hang from trees or lie in underground burrows abandoned by creatures such as fieldmice. The queen wasp mates in the autumn, then hibernates through the winter in a safe place. In spring, she builds the first cells of a new nest and lays her eggs. Her first offspring are small females called workers who enlarge the nest and defend it from intruders. As more cells are built, so the queen lays more eggs. Her last offspring, born in late summer, include both males and larger females who may themselves become queens.

1 The queen wasp selects her nest site. She builds a stalk of paper which will anchor the nest to its support.

2 The queen makes a few cells from paper and lays some eggs in them. When the eggs hatch, they become the queen's first workers.

3 The workers build a series of combs connected to each other by paper rods. Some workers build the cells, while others build the outside covering of the nest. A worker wasp uses its antennae to judge the angle and thickness of the cell walls.

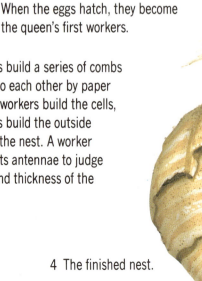

4 The finished nest.

Common wasps build their nests from paper which they make by chewing wood into pulp.

The European Water Spider

The water spider moves slowly through the still, murky water of the pond, drawing threads of silk between two underwater plants. Gradually she weaves the silken platform which will become her home. The platform built, the water spider swims to the surface. She turns a somersault, trapping a large bubble of air between her back legs. Still carrying the air bubble, the water spider swims back to her underwater home, pulling herself down the stems of the water plants with her front legs until she is underneath the platform. She opens her back legs, releasing the air bubble so that it floats upwards and becomes trapped in the silk. The spider swims towards the surface once more, to collect another bubble of air.

European water spiders spend most of their lives underwater. To help them stay underwater for long periods of time, water spiders build a kind of 'diving bell' — an underwater web filled with air. The spider pulls air bubbles down from the surface and releases them so they become trapped in the silk of the web. The spider is able to sit inside her air-filled web and wait for passing prey. Water spiders eat water insects, small fish such as minnows, and tadpoles.

1 The water spider spins a silken web between suitable water plants.

2 The spider swims to the surface to collect an air bubble.

3 The spider releases the air bubble so that it is trapped by the silk of the web.

4 The spider sits inside the air bubble, dangling her legs in the water so that she can feel the vibrations made by passing prey.

Water spiders are found only in Europe and parts of Asia.

The Masked Weaverbird

High in the banana tree, the male masked weaverbird searches for the perfect leaf with which to start his nest. He uses his beak to tear off a long, thin strip from the chosen leaf, which he then carries back to his nest site. With one foot, the weaverbird holds the strip in position on the branch and, with his beak, loops one end round the branch several times. Finally, he ties off this end of the strip by threading it through one of the loops and pulling it tight, to form a strong knot. The bird then moves along the branch and repeats the same action with the other end of the strip, so that the strip hangs under the branch like a swing. The weaverbird returns many times to the banana tree, bringing back a new leaf strip each time. With deft movements of his beak, he weaves the strips together, building up the basket shape of his nest.

Weaverbirds are found in most parts of the world. Most of them weave hanging nests, but different species create different shapes of nest and use different types of patterns and knots while weaving. The nests, which can be as large as footballs, usually have entrances on the side or in the bottom, and often have a separate egg-chamber inside. Some weaverbirds protect their nests from predators by adding a long, woven tube at the nest entrance. Weaverbirds tend to use green materials, such as reeds or strips of leaves, for their weaving, because these are more flexible.

Social weaverbirds, which live in South Africa, band together to build one giant nest. As many as 300 pairs of birds will live in the nest, which may be as large as a small motor car!

This masked weaverbird is found in East Africa. Different species of weaverbird have different skills. Some create beautiful nests, others simply gather together a few sticks and bits of straw to make a very crude home.

The Black-Tailed Prairie Dog

The coyote trots towards the thousands of burrows which make up the prairie dog township. The prairie dog sentries, sitting upright on mounds of earth at the entrances to their underground city, watch the predator carefully, making whistling barks to warn the other members of their community of the approaching danger. Some of the prairie dogs stand on their hind legs to get a better view of the intruder. Others do not wait to see what the coyote will do, but bolt for safety, vanishing into their burrows and taking refuge in the maze of tunnels and chambers they have built underground.

Black-tailed prairie dogs are members of the squirrel family. They are found on the plains of North America and southern Canada. Prairie dogs live in highly organized family groups called coteries, which usually contain one adult male, three or four females, and several young. Each coterie has its own territory with as many as 100 burrows, some of which may be five metres deep. The burrows are connected by a network of tunnels. Coteries often join together to form large colonies called townships which may contain 1,000 or more prairie dogs. Prairie dogs emerge from their burrows during the day, to graze. Sentries are always on duty, to warn the others of the approach of predators such as bobcats, coyotes and eagles.

Although an adult black-tailed prairie dog is only about 40 centimetres long, prairie dog burrows are spacious, allowing plenty of room for a group's members to move around. A typical prairie dog burrow consists of a wide shaft about one metre in diameter, tunnelled straight down into the ground to a depth of between three and five metres. Several underground tunnels branch off from the bottom of this shaft, leading to nest chambers and food stores. At the entrance to the shaft, the prairie dogs build a mound of earth to stop rainwater pouring in. Sentries use the mound as a look-out post.

Prairie dogs have long, sharp claws to help them dig easily through the soil.

The Trapdoor Spider

The female spider puts the finishing touches to the tiny burrow she has dug in the soft earth. She lines the tube-shaped nest with silk, then moves outside to make the door. She gathers tiny pieces of soil and binds them together with sticky silk, gradually creating the circular lid which will hide the entrance to her lair. She attaches the lid to the edge of the entrance with silk hinges, to make the trapdoor from which she takes her name. Finally she weights down the trapdoor by adding pieces of gravel to the inside, so that it will stay firmly in place when it is shut.

There are several species of trapdoor spider, most of which live in warm climates. Some dig simple, tube-shaped burrows, others make more complicated nests. All the burrows are well hidden. The trapdoor blends in so well with its surroundings that the spider's hidey-

hole is almost impossible to spot. The female's burrow is both a nest for rearing her young and a lair from which she ambushes passing prey. Most female trapdoor spiders never leave their burrows at all. Only when darkness falls will the spider lift the door slightly and look out. If an insect scuttles past, she grabs it and drags it inside. Male trapdoor spiders also build burrows, but they leave their homes from time to time to search for a mate.

A spider produces silk in glands inside its body. The silk, which is made of protein, begins as a liquid and passes through spinning tubes to the spinarets at the back of the spider's body. The spinarets move rather like fingers, spinning the silken threads. They can stretch out or be squeezed together to make thin thread or wide silken bands. A trapdoor spider can also use different groups of glands and spinarets to produce sticky silk for making its trap and soft silk for lining its burrow.

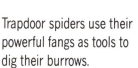

Trapdoor spiders use their powerful fangs as tools to dig their burrows.

The Mallee Fowl

A female mallee fowl will lay as many as 30 eggs during a summer. Each time she is ready to lay, the mound has to be opened up. The male will not allow the female to lay if, by opening the mound at that particular time, the temperature inside will be raised or lowered dramatically.

The male mallee fowl stands on top of the huge mound of sand which he has built among the trees. He begins to scratch furiously at the surface, using his feet to scrape sand away from the top of the pile. From time to time, he stops work and prods the sand with his beak, checking the temperature inside the mound. Then he begins scraping again until a thick surface layer has been removed. His mate climbs towards the top of the mound, ready to lay another egg, but the male darts towards her and drives her away. She must wait until it is safe to open up the mound and expose the nest. To do so now would cause a dramatic change in temperature and damage the eggs already there.

Mallee fowls live in Australia. During the winter the male digs a huge pit, over one metre deep and five metres across. He fills this with dead leaves and plants, then digs out a bowl shape in the top. In spring, after the first heavy rainfall, he covers the whole mound with sand. The dead leaves and plants begin to rot. As they rot, they warm up. When the female is ready to lay her first egg, the male clears a hole in the top of the sand. The female lays her egg, then the male covers up the hole again. The heat created by the rotting leaves keeps the eggs warm. The male tries to keep the temperature inside the mound as constant as possible, so that the eggs are not damaged before they are ready to hatch.

The male must make sure that the temperature inside the mound stays as close to 34°C as possible. He tests the temperature with his beak.

When the dead leaves and plants begin to rot, the temperature inside the mound may get too hot. The male scrapes away some of the sand to let the mound cool down.

The mound also has to be protected from the fierce heat of the sun. Sometimes the male has to heap more sand on to the mound to protect it from the sun's rays.

In late summer, when the weather gets cooler, the male must make sure that the mound does not get too cold. During the day he opens up the mound to let in the sun's heat, then covers it over at night to keep in the warmth.

When the chicks hatch, they are strong enough to dig their own way up through the mound.

The Malaysian Cave Swiftlet

The swiftlet flutters through the darkness, searching the walls of the vast cave for a suitable nesting site. Unable to see in the gloom, the swiftlet makes high-pitched clicking sounds which travel through the air. When these waves of sound hit an object, an echo bounces back towards the swiftlet. By listening to the echoes, the bird is able to tell the position of solid objects, and so can find its way around. At last it reaches a tiny ledge high up, near the cave roof. Clinging tightly to the rockface, the swiftlet opens its beak and spits sticky saliva on to the rock. It pauses to allow its enlarged glands to produce more saliva, then spits again. Using its beak, the swiftlet arranges the saliva into a horseshoe shape. The saliva dries rapidly, hardening as it does so.

The bird perches on the horseshoe framework and, moving its head from side to side, begins to build out the sides of its cup-shaped nest. It may take a month before the nest is complete.

There are probably between 15 and 20 species of swiftlet in the world, but no one is certain. Most live in India, Malaysia, Thailand and Indonesia. Swiftlets nest on the faces of sea cliffs or in dark caves. All species of swiftlet use their own sticky saliva to build their cup-shaped nests. This saliva, which is as sticky as gum, is produced by glands in the swiftlet's mouth. Some species mix the saliva with bark, feathers or plant matter, but the Malaysian cave swiftlet uses nothing but saliva. A male and female often share the building work between them.

During the day, swiftlets leave their cave homes to search for food. They feed their young on tiny insects rolled into balls and glued together with saliva. Each ball may contain as many as 500 insects.

Cave swiftlets find their way around in the darkness by using a system of sounds and echoes known as echo-location. Sounds made by the swiftlets travel through the air, sending echoes back to the birds whenever the beams of sound hit an object. By listening to the echoes, the birds can tell where the cave walls and other large objects are.

The nests of Malaysian cave swiftlets are edible, and are collected and sold to restaurants around the world. Each bird builds three nests each year, all of which are harvested. The third nest is left until the swiftlets have raised their young.

The European Common Mole

Deep underground the small, furry mammal digs furiously. Her strong front legs, armed with long, finger-like claws, cut into the soil and scoop it backwards. From time to time she tunnels up to the surface and pushes a mound of loose soil on to the ground. Soon she has hollowed out a large, round chamber which will be the centre of her nest. She then begins work on the first of a series of smaller rooms which will lead off from this central chamber. Once these are completed, the mole will dig long passageways from the nest to her feeding grounds. She works tirelessly as she tries to finish the complicated network of tunnels, chambers and escape routes that will be her home.

European moles are found in most European countries as well as in parts of Asia. They are superb builders, and can drill their way through about 15 metres of soil in an hour. Moles spend most of their lives underground, and come to the surface only when food is scarce. Their favourite food is earthworms. Sometimes a mole will store hundreds, even thousands, of worms in its underground rooms. The mole paralyses the worms with a bite, to prevent them escaping. Moles are very unsociable creatures, and mix with other moles only at mating time. They have tiny eyes, and are almost blind. Sometimes you can tell where a mole has been burrowing, because of the mounds of loose soil above ground.

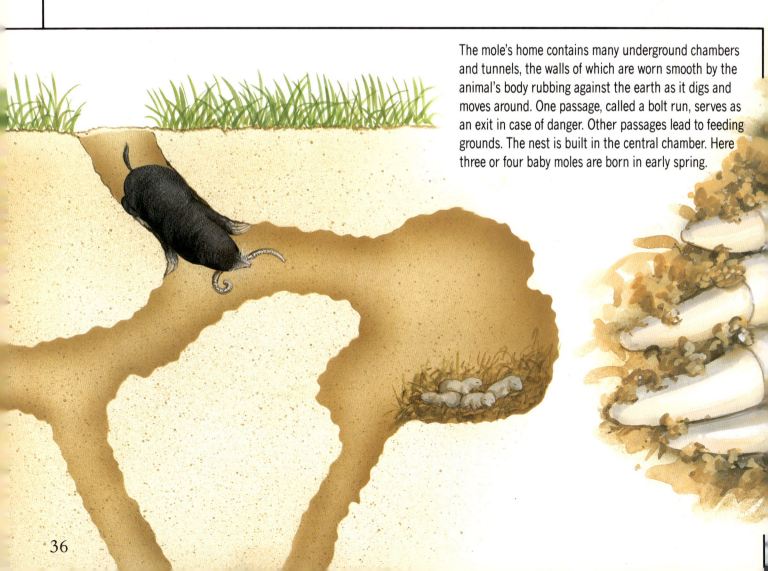

The mole's home contains many underground chambers and tunnels, the walls of which are worn smooth by the animal's body rubbing against the earth as it digs and moves around. One passage, called a bolt run, serves as an exit in case of danger. Other passages lead to feeding grounds. The nest is built in the central chamber. Here three or four baby moles are born in early spring.

A mole's front paws are ideal digging tools. The bones are short and strong, and the muscles extremely powerful. The finger-like claws cut through the soil, then the mole's paddle-like paws pull the loose earth away from, and behind, the mole's body. When digging, the mole keeps its balance by pushing its back legs into the soil and gripping firmly.

The Grey Tree Frog

The leaves of the trees are moist with water from a recent rainstorm. The female grey tree frog clings to a branch, held there safely by the suckers on her feet. Almost 10 metres below, the waters of the lake sparkle in the hazy sunlight. This is a perfect site for the grey tree frog to build her nest. She moves on to the underside of a broad leaf, and begins to lay her eggs. As she lays, she uses her back legs to whisk the mucus round the eggs into a frothy mass of foam. The outer surface of the foam dries in the sun, forming a crust which will protect the eggs and keep them moist until they develop into tadpoles.

The grey foam-nesting tree frog is found in forest and dry grassland areas of South Africa. Rain falls very rarely in these areas and so the female grey tree frog, whose eggs must be laid above water, cannot breed regularly. Instead, she must take advantage of any sudden, heavy rainstorm which fills dried-up ponds and lakes. Once the eggs are laid safely in their moist, foamy nest, they take only a few days to develop into tadpoles. As they do so, the movement of the young tadpoles within the nest causes the protective crust to break. The tadpoles drop safely into the water below. There, they grow into froglets.

The eggs develop into tadpoles after only a few days.

The movement of the hatching tadpoles causes the nest to break up, and the tadpoles fall into the water below.

The female grey tree frog may lay as many as 1,000 eggs in her nest!

The Rainbow Parrot Fish

The rays of the setting sun cast a pink glow over the reef and on the silvery bodies of the fish which cruise among the rocks. A rainbow parrot fish snatches its last meal of the day, biting off lumps of brain coral with its large, bony lips. As it feeds, the parrot fish begins to produce a sticky mucus from its body. The fish fans its tail backwards and forwards, swishing the sticky strands towards its head. After two hours, the fish is completely cocooned in its night-time nest.

The rainbow parrot fish is found near coral reefs around the coasts of North America. Every night, the rainbow parrot fish protects itself from predators by covering its body with a 'sleeping bag' of mucus. Wrapped in this protective coat, the fish can sleep in safety and without fear of being attacked by its deadly enemy, the moray eel.

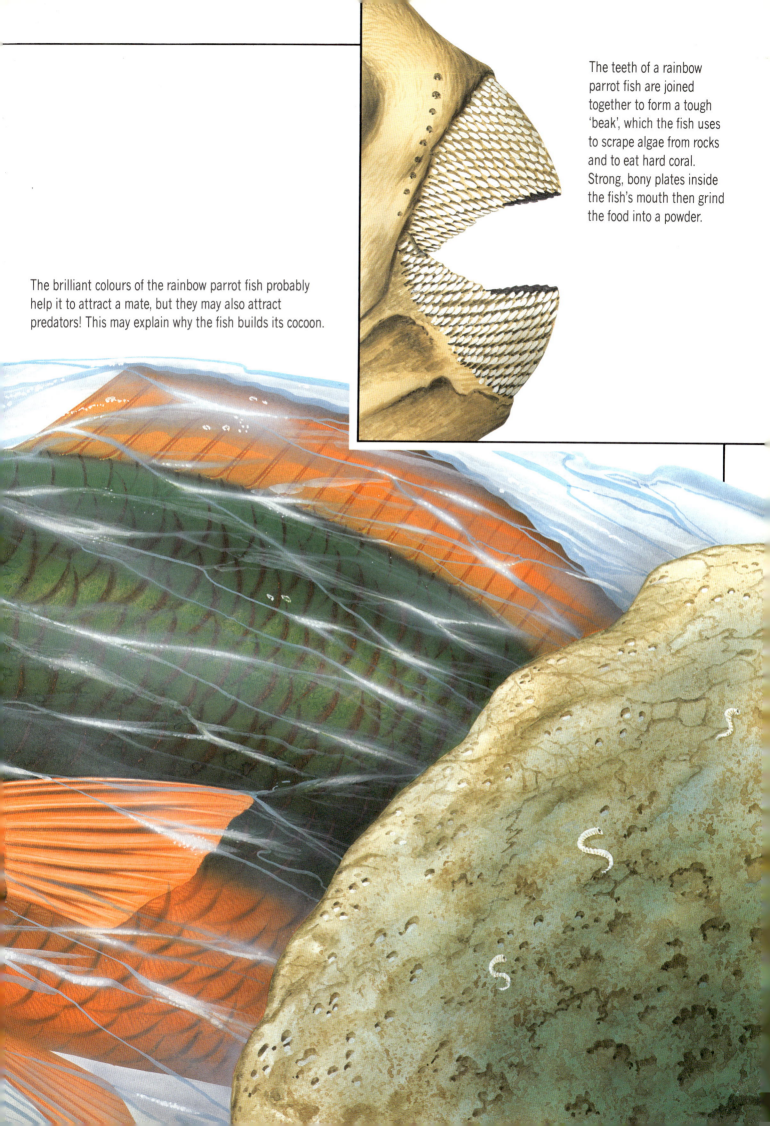

The teeth of a rainbow parrot fish are joined together to form a tough 'beak', which the fish uses to scrape algae from rocks and to eat hard coral. Strong, bony plates inside the fish's mouth then grind the food into a powder.

The brilliant colours of the rainbow parrot fish probably help it to attract a mate, but they may also attract predators! This may explain why the fish builds its cocoon.

The Southern Hairy-Nosed Wombat

The Southern hairy-nosed wombat lives in the dry scrubland of south-central Australia. The Northern hairy-nosed wombat is now very rare. Only about 20 are believed to remain in the wild, in a small woodland area in eastern Queensland.

As night falls, the ground begins to cool. The Southern hairy-nosed wombat shuffles across the scrubland which has been baked hard by the searing heat of the Australian sun. The wombat chooses a suitable spot for its new home, and begins to dig. Short, powerful front legs scrabble at the soil. Huge claws rake out the dry earth in great lumps. Strong back legs push the loose earth backwards in a shower of stones and dust. Gradually the wombat, working like a tiny, furry bulldozer, begins to disappear from view down the tunnel it is digging. It will be many nights before the warren is ready for the wombat to shelter in, out of the blistering heat of the Australian outback.

There are two species of hairy-nosed wombat, both of which are found in Australia. Wombats spend most of each day resting and keeping cool in their underground homes, emerging at night to feed on grass, roots and tree bark. Each animal lives in a maze of tunnels called a warren, which may be up to 30 metres in length. A warren usually has several entrances and inside chambers. Sometimes a warren may connect with the warren of a neighbouring wombat, but wombats are usually solitary creatures who prefer to live alone.

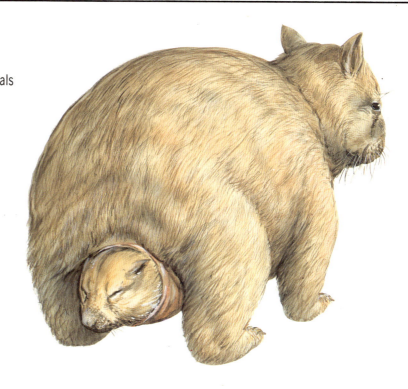

Wombats are marsupials, one of a group of mammals found only in Australia. Adult female marsupials have pouches on their bodies, in which they carry their young. The opening of a female wombat's pouch is at the rear of her body. This allows the female to dig and burrow while carrying her cub.

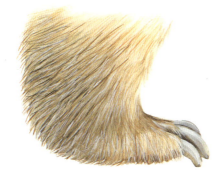

An adult wombat is about one metre long. Its strong, powerful legs and the massive claws on its front feet are perfectly designed for tunnelling through soil.

The Potter Wasp

Hidden in the undergrowth, the female potter wasp gathers a pellet of mud from a patch of wet ground then flies back to her chosen nest site nearby. Her front legs and mandibles mould the pellet into a long strip which she lays carefully on the ground in a ring.

The female potter wasp regurgitates water from her stomach to make each mud pellet soft enough to shape easily. When she has finished the nest, she seals it with a stopper made from the last pellet.

She returns to the mud patch many times, until she has gathered enough pellets to build a bottle-shaped nest. The nest is a perfect storage jar for a paralysed caterpillar, and a newly laid egg. When the egg hatches, the caterpillar will be its first meal.

There are thousands of species of wasp, all of which are expert nest-builders. 'Social wasps', so-called because they live in colonies, build nests from paper which they make by chewing wood fibres into a pulp. But most wasps live by themselves. The females of these 'solitary wasps' do all the work of nest-building. Usually the nest is dug underground, but some solitary wasps, such as the potter wasp, build their nests above ground. Many species of solitary wasps are parasitic. The female uses her stinger to paralyse her prey, then lays her eggs in or on its body.

A wasp's body has three parts: a head, a thorax and an abdomen. On its head are two compound eyes, each made up of many tiny lenses; two antennae which are sensitive to smell and touch; and mouthparts for chewing food and sucking up liquids. Wings and legs are connected to the thorax, the middle part of a wasp's body. A wasp's abdomen contains its stomach. Female wasps have a stinger hidden near the end of the abdomen.

1 The potter wasp carries another pellet of mud to her bottle-shaped nest.

2 The completed nest.

3 The potter wasp places her egg inside the finished nest, along with a caterpillar she has captured and paralysed. The caterpillar is supplied as food for the egg when it develops into a larva, or 'grub'. The larva will reach full size in between seven and 20 days, depending on the species and on the weather. It then spins a covering called a cocoon. While it is in the cocoon, the larva becomes a pupa.

4 The pupa stage is the one during which the insect becomes an adult. At the end of the pupa stage, the adult breaks out of the cocoon and out of the nest.

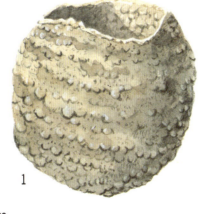

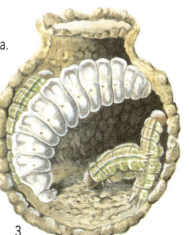

The 'Gardening' Ant

The sky is full of flying ants as the young queens and winged males swarm high in the air on their one and only mating flight. Soon the cloud of leafcutter ants begins to thin. The queens fly off to find suitable nesting sites, and the males sink to the ground to die. One queen lands near a rotten tree stump and tears off her wings with her strong jaws. Her wings are no longer useful — she will never fly again. She crawls into a crack in the dry ground under the tree's roots. Here she finds a hollow chamber and carefully drops on to the floor the pellet of fungus she has carried from the old nest. She seals the entrance of her new nest with earth and begins to lay the first of the many thousands of eggs which will hatch out to become her colony.

There are about 14,000 species of ant. Some live by hunting and raiding. Others live by a kind of farming. Among these are the 'gardeners', such as the leafcutter ants of North and South America. Leafcutter ants live in gigantic colonies. Their nest is a mound of earth dotted with hundreds, even thousands, of tiny entrances. Inside the nest, which can be six metres deep, is a maze of tunnels and chambers. Many of the chambers are gardens for growing a fungus which the adult ants eat and use to feed their larvae. The ants cut and gather leaves for the fungus to grow on, and they fertilise the fungus with fluids from their bodies. The ants devote their whole lives to looking after the fungus, constantly weeding out any unwelcome fungi which start to grow.

Large workers cut out pieces of leaf with their sharp jaws. The workers carry the pieces to the nest. They hold them in their jaws, but raise them above their heads like umbrellas. They drop the pieces at the entrance to the nest and return for more.

Smaller workers collect the pieces. They lick them clean and cut them up into smaller pieces.

They chew the leaf pieces into a pulp. They feed the fungus with this pulp.

Glossary and Index

abdomen The rear section of an insect's body. The abdomen contains the insect's stomach.

antennae Two long, thin 'feelers' found on the heads of some insects. Antennae are used for smelling and touching.

camouflage Any special shape or colouring which disguises a creature or helps it to hide from its enemies.

cocoon A protective covering, usually spun from silk by an insect at the end of its larval stage. Other creatures, such as the rainbow parrot fish, spin a cocoon from mucus.

colony A group of animals which live together in an organized way. Each member of the group has a particular job to do, and there are rules to follow.

fry The name given to young fish which have just developed from eggs.

hibernate To sleep or remain inactive during the cold winter months, when food is scarce.

larvae The name given to young insects in their first stage of growth. The larval stage lasts from the time the insect leaves the egg until it becomes a pupa.

mandibles The name given to an insect's pair of jaws.

mucus A slimy liquid which is made inside the body of some animals.

predator A creature which lives by hunting other animals for food.

pupae The name given to young insects after they have passed through the larval stage. Pupae develop into adult insects.

thorax The middle section of an insect's body.

---

abdomen 45, 48
ant 5, 12, 13, 46, 47
   'gardening' ant 46, 47
   weaver ant 12, 13
antennae 13, 22, 45, 48

beak 5, 8, 20, 26, 33, 34, 41
beaver, North American 6, 7
bowerbird 20, 21
   MacGregor's bowerbird 21
   satin bowerbird 20, 21
   tooth-billed bowerbird 21
burrow 22, 28, 29, 30, 31, 43

caddis fly 14, 15
   caddis fly larva 14, 15
camouflage 14, 48
cave swiftlet, Malaysian 34, 35
chamber 7, 8, 10, 26, 28, 29, 36, 43, 46
chicks 9, 33
claws 5, 12, 29, 36, 37, 43
cocoon 41, 45, 48
colony 5, 11, 12, 22, 45, 46, 48
compound eyes 45
coterie 28

dam 6, 7

earth 5, 10, 21, 28, 29, 30, 36, 37, 43, 46
echo-location 34
eggs 5, 8, 9, 10, 15, 16, 17, 22, 26, 32, 33, 38, 39, 45, 46, 48

fangs 31
food 5, 7, 10, 15, 29, 34, 36, 41, 45

frog, grey tree 38, 39
fry 16, 17, 48
fungus 46

glands 5, 14, 18, 31, 34
grub 45, 48

hibernate 22, 48

incisors 7
insect 12, 18, 24, 31, 34, 45, 48

jaws 6, 12, 13, 46, 48

larva(e) 10, 12, 13, 14, 15, 45, 46, 48
lodge 7

mallee fowl 32, 33
mandibles 13, 44, 48
mate 5, 20, 31, 33, 41
mole, European common 36, 37
mound 6, 10, 11, 16, 28, 29, 32, 33, 36, 46
mouth 7, 14, 16, 17, 34
mouthparts 22, 45
mucus 38, 40, 48
mud 6, 7, 8, 22, 44, 45

nest 5, 8, 9, 10, 12, 13, 16, 17, 18, 22, 23, 26, 27, 29, 30, 31, 33, 34, 35, 36, 38, 39, 40, 44, 45, 46

prairie dog, black-tailed 28, 29
predator 8, 14, 26, 28, 40, 41, 48
prey 5, 18, 24, 31, 45
pupa 45, 48

rainbow parrot fish 40, 41

Rufous ovenbird 8, 9

saliva 5, 10, 20, 22, 34
silk 5, 12, 13, 14, 18, 19, 24, 30, 31
spider 5, 18, 19, 24, 25, 30, 31
   European water spider 24, 25
   orb-weaver spider 18, 19
   trapdoor spider 30, 31
spinarets 31
stickleback, three-spined 16, 17
stinger 45
stomach 16, 44, 45

tadpoles 24, 38
teeth 5, 6, 7, 41
termite 5, 10, 11
   magnetic termite 10, 11
territory 16, 28
thorax 45, 48
trap 5, 18, 24, 31
tunnel 5, 7, 10, 16, 17, 28, 29, 36, 43, 46

wasp 5, 22, 23, 44, 45
   common wasp 22, 23
   potter wasp 44, 45
   'social' wasps 22, 45
   'solitary' wasps 45
weaverbird 26, 27
   masked weaverbird 26, 27
   social weaverbird 26
web 18, 19, 24
wombat 42, 43
   Northern hairy-nosed wombat 42
   Southern hairy-nosed wombat 42, 43